DRINK *like a* LOCAL
MIAMI

*A Field Guide to
Miami's Best Bars*

Drink Like a Local: Miami
A Field Guide to Miami's Best Bars

13-Digit ISBN: 978-1-64643-012-3
10-Digit ISBN: 1-64643-012-3

This book may be ordered by mail from the publisher. Please include $5.99 for postage and handling. Please support your local bookseller first!

Books published by Cider Mill Press Book Publishers are available at special discounts for bulk purchases in the United States by corporations, institutions, and other organizations. For more information, please contact the publisher.

Cider Mill Press Book Publishers
"Where good books are ready for press"
501 Nelson Place
Nashville, Tennessee 37214

cidermillpress.com

Typography: Ballinger, Condor, Pacifico, Poppins, Stolzl

Printed in China
23 24 25 26 27 TYC 5 4 3 2 1
First Edition

DRINK *like a* LOCAL
MIAMI

*A Field Guide to
Miami's Best Bars*

AMBER LOVE BOND

CIDER MILL
PRESS

BOOK
PUBLISHERS

CONTENTS

As a Miami native, I know a thing or two about the 305. Growing up in Miami I experienced its transition from the home of the cocaine cowboys (a bit before my time, but the stories are still told) to it being the place where you came to lounge on the beach all day and club all night to being the cultural mecca of amazing hospitality that it is today. Over the last decade or so, Miami has blossomed into a city that's finally being taken seriously for its food and drink scenes.

From being recognized by the prestigious Michelin Guide to being home to one of the best dive bars in the country, Miami is a place of excitement and nostalgia that never grows old for the locals who live and love in the Magic City. For me, sitting at the very bars and restaurants featured in this book, I found a community and a passion for telling the stories of those who stir and shake some of the best cocktails in town. Drinking like a local here means embracing all that encompasses the most well-known city in the Sunshine State.

This city was founded on opportunity, after the "Mother of Miami," Julia Tuttle, alongside Mary Brickell, success-fully convinced Henry Flagler to extend the East Coast Railway down to the end of Florida's coast because they were so confident it would become a hub for agriculture, travel, and, ultimately, growth.

On July 28, 1896, Miami was officially incorporated. Through the Great Depression and the Great Miami Hurricane of 1926, the region continued to be as resilient as its many palm trees. World War II brought permanent residents who decided to call Miami home. The city grew. When Fidel Castro brought Communism to Cuba, many Cubans moved to Miami, and to this day Miami still has the largest population of Cuban Americans in the U.S. Miami is a melting pot of different cultures, races, and religions from completely different walks of life that unite in a special way under bright sunny skies.

Drink Like a Local: Miami is not just about sipping great cocktails—it is a trip down memory lane. The focus of this book is not only on historical dives or temples of craft cocktails—Miami has loads of both—it's on the everyday places Miamians go to enjoy a beer after work or to see their favorite bartender or meet friends.

Our melting pot of cultures gives us a look into what it must have been like to live in a different era. Take, for example, Mac's Club Deuce (see page 24). Mac Klein served in World War II, made his way down to Miami, bought the bar in 1964, and ran the legendary spot until his death at 101 years old. Or the story of Cantinero Julio Cabrera, who came to Miami from Castro's Cuba to create a better life for his family. He eventually opened one of the best bars in the world, Café La Trova (see page 146). And you can't discuss the restaurant culture in Miami without mentioning Flanigan's, which has been serving hungry Miamians since 1959 (see page 102).

No matter where you go, you're not going to go thirsty, and chances are you're going to soak in some amazing Biscayne Bay blues along the way.

MIAMI

Miami Beach/South Beach

A. Broken Shaker
2727 Indian Creek Drive

B. Sweet Liberty Bar & Supply Co.
237 20th Street Suite B

C. Bay Club
1930 Bay Road

D. The Abbey Brewing Company
1115–1117 16th Street

E. Tropezón
512 Española Way

F. Lost Weekend
218 Española Way

G. Mac's Club Deuce
222 14th Street

H. Swizzle Rum Bar & Drinkery
1120 Collins Avenue

I. Mezcalista
921 Washington Avenue

J. Macchialina
820 Alton Road

K. Minibar
418 Meridian Avenue

L. Orilla
426 Euclid Avenue

M. Ted's Hideaway
124 2nd Street

BROKEN SHAKER

2727 Indian Creek Drive
Miami Beach, FL 33140

As one of the first Miami bar programs to be recognized nationally (by both James Beard and World's 50 Best), it's no surprise that Broken Shaker is on every local's beloved bar list. Owned by Gabe Orta and Elad Zvi of Bar Lab, this spot engulfs everything we love about Miami. It's one of those tropical and tranquilo spots that serves fun cocktails on an ever-changing list.

Let's set the scene: you walk into a kind of musty smelling hostel, not sure what you're going to find, but once you make it through to the courtyard you're welcomed with palm trees, cozy couches, and a pool that's open to the public. The cocktails are creative and tasty and the food by chef Jimmy Lebron is worldy, yet still so Miami—think Haitian griot and pikliz and guac with tostones. Broken Shaker now has locations in New York, Chicago, and Los Angeles, but the OG Miami spot is forever a favorite.

SWEET LIBERTY BAR & SUPPLY CO.

237 20th Street Suite B,
Miami Beach, FL 33139

Happy hour oysters, coffee-infused pina coladas, and James Beard award-winning food until 4 a.m. every day are just some of the magical things that make guests obsessed with this South Beach mainstay. The "Pursue Happiness" neon welcomes thirsty friends and makes for the perfect backdrop while dancing the night away until the wee hours of the morning.

Bartenders here are some of the best in the country—in fact, they've been recognized as Best Bar Team and Best Bar by Tales of the Cocktail foundation on more than one occasion. Behind the bar you'll find one singular table that gets the best view of all the action. Though it's most often full of local bartenders or other industry friends hanging out, it is open to anyone who calls ahead and requests a reservation at the "bar table." The first Sunday of the month you'll find a Fruit Cocktail drag brunch that takes the already delicious brunch menu (think bourbon chicken and waffles) to an entirely different level.

JOHN LERMAYER'S PIÑA COLADA

You haven't had a piña colada until you've had the one served at Sweet Liberty. A signature cocktail of the late, great John Lermayer, a top bartender and owner of this hot spot who passed away a few years ago, it's so popular that other industry-facing bars have added it to their menu in his honor.

2 oz. rum (Sweet Liberty uses a secret blend of Jamaican overproof and Venezuelan rums)

2 oz. fresh pineapple juice

1 oz. Coco Real

¼ oz. fresh lemon juice

3 coffee beans

½ oz. Lustau PX Sherry, to float

1. Combine all of the ingredients, except the sherry, in a blender with ice, blend, and pour into a hurricane glass.

2. Float the sherry on top and garnish with a maraschino cherry, flamingo pick, umbrella, and mint bouquet.

BAY CLUB

1930 Bay Road
Miami Beach, FL 33139

Sunset Harbour is one of those neighborhoods that has everything within reach, no need to step foot into a car. Naturally, in an area like this you're bound to find a chill bar where locals know they can grab a drink, hang with friends, and always have a great time.

At Bay Club, you've got just that. Drinks are solid and pizza from neighboring Lucali is served until midnight. Happy hour tends to be a little more relaxed, but the party amps up as it gets later with comedy nights, live music, and karaoke.

THE ABBEY BREWING COMPANY

1115–1117 16th Street
Miami Beach, FL 33139

The first craft beer bar to grace Miami Beach, Abbey Brewing Company opened in 1995 and has happily become a landmark for those wanting an ice-cold beer and a chance to escape the craziness of Ocean Drive. While there is a full liquor bar, the beers are the real stars of the show.

Owner and brewmaster Raymond Rigazio opened The Abbey as an homage to the monks who brewed beer in the Middle Ages. We're eternally thankful he left the corporate world for the sands of Miami Beach to brew some beer.

MIAMI BEACH/SOUTH BEACH

19

TROPEZÓN

512 Española Way
Miami Beach, FL 33139

Looking for a gin & tonic to help save you from Miami's heat? Well, this Andalusian bar has just the fix as their menu features several different versions and lots of infused-specialty gins. Tucked into a hidden historical corridor of Española Way, you'll feel immediately transported to Spain at this spot. You're going to want to order the acorn-fed Jamon Iberico de Bellota, but you really can't go wrong with any of their tapas.

Tropezón is housed in Esmé, which is described as "a window onto the halcyon days of hustlers that played 'em as they laid, artists that dared to break the mold, and It girls that left their beauty mark on the styles of the times."

TROPEZON NEGRONI

1 oz. Gin Mare

1 oz. Peychaud Aperitif

¾ oz. sweet vermouth

1 bar spoon Pedro Ximenez Sherry

4 drops saline solution

1. Combine all of the ingredients in a mixing glass with ice, stir until properly diluted, and strain into a rocks glass over a large ice cube.

2. Express an orange peel over the glass and garnish the drink with the expressed peel and an orange slice.

LOST WEEKEND

218 Española Way
Miami Beach, FL 33139

Inspired by John Lennon's "lost weekend" period, an eighteen-month stretch in the mid-1970s when Lennon was separated from Yoko Ono and during which he caroused with the likes of Harry Nilsson, this has been one of Miami Beach's mainstay dive bars since 1996. It offers a small food menu, including Philly cheesesteaks courtesy of The Alibi, while serving cold beers and simple cocktails.

It's one of those spots that feels a bit like a fever dream. You'll find yourself singing along to every song that plays, while simultaneously convincing yourself that you're a pool shark who definitely needs another shot of tequila. If you lose anything here, it just might be a few hours of sleep you thought you were going to get, but were having way too much fun to care.

MAC'S CLUB DEUCE

222 14th Street
Miami Beach, FL 33139

Miami Vice cast parties went down here; Anthony Bourdain said it was one of his favorite spots in the world; and in 2010, *Playboy* named it one of the "best dive bars" in America, as did *Vice*, later. Referred to as simply The Deuce by locals, this is Miami's oldest—and possibly smokiest—bar. At any given time you'll find locals, visitors, and plenty of industry folks looking to decompress after a long day. It opened in 1926 and was owned by Mac Klein until 1964 when he passed away at 101 years old.

The secret to his old age? Perhaps the legendary 2-for-1 happy hour that takes place daily from 8 a.m. to 5 p.m. It's cash only and if the bar thinks you've had enough, they'll quietly give you a card that reads:

YOU HAVE JUST BEEN
86'D
LEAVE QUIETLY
AND NO ONE WILL KNOW
IT'S BEEN A PLEASURE TO SERVE YOU.

SWIZZLE RUM BAR & DRINKERY

1120 Collins Avenue
Miami Beach, FL 33139

Many consider Danilo "Dacha" Bozovic, the barkeep at Swizzle, one of the best bartenders in the world. Bozovic focuses on rum as he takes his guests on a journey through a menu of forgotten classics and reinventions in this speakeasy that sits below the Stiles Hotel. If you blink, you might miss it. Pro tip: sit in front of Bozovic at the bar and watch him work.

An author of more than one cocktail book, he knows his way around spirits and is always happy to lead guests through rum tastings as the bar boasts over 100 different types within the cozy space.

RHUM SWIZZLE

The funky rhum plays with the Watermelon Shrub in this Danilo Bozovic cocktail—a perfect summer sipper.

1½ oz. Rhum JM 100 Proof

1 oz. Watermelon Shrub

½ oz. fresh lime juice

½ oz. simple syrup

½ oz. pineapple juice

1. Place all of the ingredients and some pebble ice in a tiki glass.

2. Stir in glass until blended and chilled.

3. Add more ice to top and garnish with a watermelon slice.

Watermelon Shrub: Combine the juice from 1 pressed watermelon with equal parts apple cider vinegar and sugar (usually 2 cups vinegar and 2 cups sugar).

MEZCALISTA

921 Washington Avenue
Miami, FL 33139

Whether you're obsessed with mezcal or wanting to learn more, this mezcal bar and tasting room is a spot you should definitely check out. You might need help finding this drinking den located deep inside Moxy Hotel, but once inside you'll discover a bar that features over 100 mezcals, with an emphasis on producers that practice environmental sustainability. It's Miami Beach's only mezcaleria, and it doubles as a lounge and bar with weekend DJs and bottle service.

Designed by Saladino Design Studios, and run by the team behind the Miami staple Coyo Taco, Mezcalista houses a cozy atmosphere during the week and gets a bit more upbeat and high energy toward the end of the week. Because what's a party without a bit of quality mezcal?

MACCHIALINA

820 Alton Road
Miami Beach, FL 33139

It's a family affair at Macchialina and that's just part of what makes this spot a favorite for Miami locals. Located in the heart of South Beach's West Avenue neighborhood, Macchialina is known for it's mouth-watering Italian fare by chef Mike Pirolo and absolutely bonkers wine list by his sister Jacqueline Pirolo, who is recognized as one of the city's best sommeliers.

Since the pandemic they've expanded to have an outdoor oasis referred to as Il Giardino and transformed a
section of their cozy restaurant into a wine shop. There's
something special about indulging on a fabulous Italian
feast paired with great cocktails and wine, and then
knowing you can take a bottle (or two) of that very same
wine home with you.

BIG TROUBLE IN LITTLE CHIANTO SPRITZ

Spritzes are an ideal Miami cocktail. This low-ABV
concoction can be made quickly and assembled in the glass.
Share this one with friends or enjoy at Macchialina.

1 oz. Giulio Cocchi

1 oz. Barolo Chianto

2 oz. Q Grapefruit Soda

1 oz. Lovo Prosecco

1. Combine all of the ingredients in a wine glass, add ice, and
   stir to blend.
2. Add a grapefruit twist.

MINIBAR

418 Meridian Avenue
Miami Beach, FL 33139

Located just above the lobby of Urbanica Meridian Hotel, this snug little nook is exactly what it sounds like—a very small bar where, as a fun play on its name, several of the drinks are served with an actual mini bottle of spirits. That's not the only creative aspect behind the fun cocktail menu at Minibar.

The menu rotates seasonally, but every rendition is Miami-themed, making it extra special to locals who know their way around town. From cocktails named after neighborhoods to drinks inspired by iconic dishes and chefs at popular restaurants, it's all about the love of the 305 at this tropical-themed hot spot.

ORILLA

426 Euclid Avenue
Miami Beach, FL 33139

When you think of typical South Beach, the idea of an Argentinian steakhouse disguised as a tropical oasis might not come to mind, but that's exactly what Orilla is. Right off the busy 5th Street and Euclid Avenue corner of the South of Fifth neighborhood is a sneaky little spot that's easy to miss. Serving large steaks, tasty empanadas, and paella—the bar program is a true hidden gem. From tableside martinis accompanied by a five minute presentation to a Negroni with smoked pancetta, everything here is a surprise and delight.

The bartenders are friendly and excited to share their talents with those who sit at the bar. Ideal for dinners for a group or even first dates, this is one of those Miami secrets you'll want to keep in your back pocket.

FOGÓN

1 oz. Santa Teresa 1796

¾ oz. Select Aperitivo

1 oz. rectified pineapple

1 oz. Sicilian lemon juice

¼ oz. agave nectar

1. Combine all of the ingredients in a cocktail shaker with tons of ice, shake it angrily, like it's the last bit of ketchup in a glass bottle, and then double strain into a Collins glass over a big chunk of ice.

2. Burn only one side of an orange wedge until it's black and garnish.

TED'S HIDEAWAY

124 2nd Street
Miami Beach, FL 33139

Ted's Hideaway is iconic in its own right. This dive is known for being where the locals go to hide. From what? The heat, South Beach tourists, their crazy ex-girlfriend—it doesn't matter, everyone is welcome at Ted's Hideaway. Even first timers instantly feel at home in this dark, cozy spot.

Lined with televisions and bartenders who are quick to pop open a beer, you'll find plenty of options on this menu. The all day happy hour is a nice bonus and they've got all the bar food classics like hot wings, nachos, burgers, and more.

North Miami Beach

A. Shuckers
1819 79th Street Causeway

B. Happy's Stork Lounge & Liquor
1872 79th Street Causeway

C. Bob's Your Uncle
928 71st Street

D. On the Rocks Bar
217 71st Street

E. Champagne Bar at the Surf Club
9011 Collins Avenue

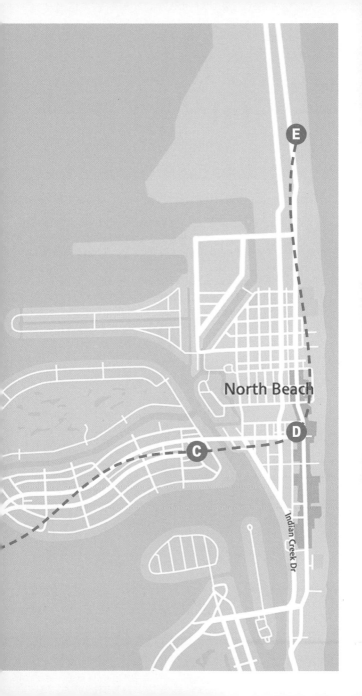

SHUCKERS

1819 79th Street Causeway
North Bay Village, FL 33141

No frills, nothing fancy, just ice-cold drinks and undefeated bay views are what you're getting at Shuckers. You may drive up and wonder if you're in the right place when your map leads you to a shabby looking Best Western at a random spot in North Bay Village, but don't worry—you're in the right place. This super chill come-as-you-are bar sits on the water with seats that go right down the wooden dock for ample bay breezes and blue waters.

Buckets of beer and literally anything fried are the move here, but really it's all pretty solid as far as bar food goes. There's a pool table, cheap happy hour, and many televisions. Open from 7:30 a.m. until midnight every day, they serve breakfast, lunch, and dinner and are family friendly.

HAPPY'S STORK LOUNGE & LIQUOR

1872 79th Street Causeway
North Bay Village, FL 33141

One of Miami's legendary dive bars, Happy's is a regular haunt for locals and hospitality industry folks who know a thing or two about what makes a bar great. Honestly, if you haven't had to drag a friend or a parent out of this bar at 5 a.m. then you can't quite call yourself a true Miamian.

Located in North Bay Village in a semi-sketchy strip mall, this is the kind of spot that makes you crave a Miller High Life. Filled with people who are looking for an easy, no frills bar to hang out in, there's a pool table, a juke box, and $4 drinks during the all-day happy hour.

The fact that it's also a liquor store that's open until 5 a.m. every day is a major bonus—it's the latest you can buy bottles of booze in town.

BOB'S YOUR UNCLE

928 71st Street
Miami Beach, FL 33141

Located in North Miami Beach's Normandy Isle, Bob's Your Uncle is a quintessential neighborhood bar, and that's just what co-owner Danielle Savin set out to do. The original Bob's calls New York its home, but while Savin was on vacation with her business partner and friends staying in this area of the beach, they found themselves wishing there was a Bob's nearby to hang out at. It didn't take long for Bob's Your Uncle Miami to appear on the scene.

Just to make sure you never forget where you are, the bar features a large wall adorned with framed images of notable Bobs—Bob Saget, Bob Dylan, Bob Hope, Bob Fosse, and even Bob the Builder.

Good people. Good drinks. Good fun. The generous pours for tasty cocktails made with locally-owned brands, along with delicious bar snacks, keep the regulars coming back. From the Bob's Old Fashioned made with salt bitters to the selection of daily Jell-o shots in unexpected flavors like banana creme and peanut butter whiskey, this isn't your average dive bar.

Pro tip: it's right next to Katana, a sushi spot known for not taking reservations and having long waits, but those waits are made much easier when you're hanging out at Bob's.

ON THE ROCKS BAR

217 71st Street
Miami Beach, FL 33141

What's special about this North Beach staple that has been serving the locals for years is that there isn't anything special about it. It's open until 5 a.m. every day of the year, even on holidays when everything else is closed. It's part sports bar, part music hall with the regular appearance of bands who play nothing but classic rock covers and karaoke on Friday nights.

You can always count on finding a good selection of beer and spirits that won't break the bank. The walls feature signs and posters that are just as unique as the guests you'll find sitting at the bar. On The Rocks is definitely one of those places where you'll find yourself coming in solo and leaving with new friends.

CHAMPAGNE BAR AT THE SURF CLUB

9011 Collins Avenue
Surfside, FL 33154

If it's not obvious by the name, this is Miami's ultimate treat-yourself bar. Located at the prestigious Four Seasons Surf Club, it's home to the largest collection of Champagne in town. A chic Italian vibe awaits guests and instantly transports you to the Amalfi Coast. The emerald-green bar is surrounded by a large lounge area and is considered the property's lobby bar just off the Lido at Surf Club Restaurant.

The cocktail menu changes seasonally but always has some kind of elaborate story to tell—whether it's about the bar team's insane trip to Italy or inspired by party invitations for the massive bashes held in the hotel in the 1950s. Be prepared to drop some cash, these cocktails are on the pricier side— think $25 per drink, but they are well worth it.

Brickell

A. RedBar Brickell
52 SW 10th Street

B. Blackbird Ordinary
729 SW 1st Avenue

C. Better Days
75 SE 6th Street

D. Baby Jane
500 Brickell Avenue #105E

E. The River Oyster Bar
33 SE 7th Street, Suite 100

F. Mo Bar
500 Brickell Key Drive

Downtown
Miami

A B C D E F

REDBAR BRICKELL

52 SW 10th Street
Miami, FL 33130

One of the longest standing bars in the ever-changing Brickell landscape, Redbar has been around since the days when the area only had one Starbucks. For those who have watched Brickell grow into the yuppie-filled metropolis it is, this has always been one of those spots you could count on to make you feel like you're at home. Maybe it's the board games and the neon lights, but this bar gives off major rec-room vibes.

The Insta-worthy "you are exactly where you need to be" neon sign has been a staple background to many late nights out as it was one of the very first craft cocktail bars in the neighborhood. From late night DJs to Whiskey Wednesday specials and comedy nights, this spot is just as lively as it was the day it first opened.

BLACKBIRD ORDINARY

729 SW 1st Avenue
Miami, FL 33130

Blackbird Ordinary is a Brickell staple that's been around since before the area's building boom. It's survived the crazy growth around their humble space with class, though the outdoor patio had to be converted to an indoor space to accommodate all the of constant construction surrounding it. OG Miamians who used to dance their cares away on the patio remember how closely the cranes would dangle as Brickell City Centre was being built.

Serving a great selection of spirts and upbeat vibes, this bar is the brainchild of Miami hospitality legend Dan Binkiewicz, who is responsible for bringing some of the city's best cocktail bars to life. The light up dance floor serves as an ode to the now defunct, greatly missed Purdy Lounge—another of Bink's bars. The late-night crowd here tends to be on the younger side and it's not unusual to find a line to get in that wraps around the block.

BLACKBIRD

The Blackbird is one of its signature cocktails and is perfect to sip. The tea and blackberry go perfect together.

2 oz. Sweet Tea Vodka

½ oz. blackberry puree

¾ oz. fresh lemon juice

¾ oz. simple syrup

1. Place all of the ingredients in a cocktail shaker with ice, shake well, and then strain into a pint glass.

2. Add pebble ice* to the glass and garnish with blackberry and mint.

*If pebble ice isn't available, use crushed ice.

BETTER DAYS

75 SE 6th Street
Miami, FL 33131

The vintage vibe of this laid-back Brickell spot is a hit with locals as well as bartenders from all over the city. Everyone in the know is happy to see Brickell's first pop-up bar now permanently residing in a proper building. Better Days acts like that neighborhood bar that doesn't focus on craft cocktails, but in actuality it takes a fresh look at craft cocktails and beers. With a nod to the past through its vintage furniture and styling, Better Days looks to bring back those chill vibes to cocktail bars while making the locals happy. The bar's main focus is customer service and the guest experience. And it really shows. Catch Will Thompson walking throughout the bar focusing on guest satisfaction. He not only runs the joint but is a local who cares about elevating cocktails in a Miami way—even though there's no actual cocktail menu. Better Days is open every day until 5 a.m.

CLOTHED & UNKNOWN

¾ oz. Bosscal Mezcal

¾ oz. Yellow Chartreuse

¾ oz. Aperol

¾ oz. fresh lemon juice

1. Place all of the ingredients in a cocktail shaker with ice, shake well, and strain into a chilled coupe.
2. Garnish with a lemon peel.

BABY JANE

500 Brickell Avenue, #105E
Miami, FL 33131

Picture this: it's late night and you're hungry, but you don't want to just grab fast food on the way home and you're still in the mood to drink. We've all been there, and Baby Jane is the answer. Open until 3 a.m. on weekdays and 5 a.m. on the weekend, this bar is not only home to great bartenders and cocktails, but a full menu of Asian deliciousness.

Dumplings, fried rice, and ramen all served hot, fresh, and fast while you sip on your drink and vibe along with the DJ. There's lots of personality packed into this small space—from the semi-open kitchen pass to a neon that reads "I'll Have What She's Having," to creatively framed women's panties on the bathroom walls.

THE RIVER OYSTER BAR

33 SE 7th Street, Suite 100
Miami, FL 33131

The oysters here are the key to River Oyster Bar's success over the last two decades. Though they've moved spaces, their new digs offer more space and an expanded menu, but the high quality of the seafood and service remains the same.

Locals know to hit this happy hour for fresh oysters and generous drink specials—hello, $8 martinis.

Bar management here places a large focus on educating their staff weekly so they are able to talk guests through questions about the cuisine, wine list, and spirits. They also do their best to keep things local by sourcing grass-fed beef from Florida, heirloom tomatoes and honey from Homestead, microgreens from Hollywood, local shrimp from Cape Canaveral, and stone crabs from the Florida Keys.

MO BAR

500 Brickell Key Drive
Miami, FL 33131

There's not much to do on Brickell Key if you're not one of the residents. But it is home to the Mandarin Oriental hotel, which is where you'll find Mo Bar. Yes, it's the hotel's lobby bar, but it's also got one of the best skyline views in the city and a happy hour that's so great, locals often keep this secret to themselves—$7 classic cocktails with a bit of a Miami riff? Yes please.

With super tall ceilings and a glamorous backbar that's parallel with Biscayne Bay and bustling Brickell, there's no shortage of stunning views at this bar that boasts large leather chairs and affordably priced bites with options like sliders and some of the best sushi around. There's live music a few nights a week that makes it tough to ever want to leave. Plus, for those who love to be star struck—this hotel is a favorite for celebs who want to stay under the radar... just don't say we're the ones who told you.

Downtown Miami

istoryM

Pérez Art Museum

Museum of Science

Freedom Tower

Kie... Church

Museum

Downtown
Miami

MIKE'S AT VENETIA

555 NE 15th Street, 9th Floor
Miami, FL 33132

Family-owned and operated for nearly two decades by Mike and Norma Shelow, this well-loved hang for hospitality professionals also happens to be considered one of the country's best sports bars.

Don't let the address fool you. You'll enter through a residential building and head up to the ninth floor to find it. But once you've made your way in, you'll be greeted by great views on the outdoor patio and a homey bar where you'll find regulars playing pool, watching a game, or chowing down on hearty bar food.

The menu features more than just your average items. Sure, there's saucy buffalo wings, jalapeño poppers, and mozzarella sticks, but there's also French onion soup, NY sirloin, and seafood fra diavlo. There are also specials every day, and $10 buckets often make an appearance on game days.

THE CORNER

1035 N Miami Avenue, #101
Miami, FL 33136

This area of the city is known for having operational licenses that allow the sale of liquor 24/7. So, needless to say, there's a lot going on here. At The Corner it's not out of the ordinary to find a scruffy dude carrying a six-foot snake charging people $5 to hold it for a photo, or bartenders trying to have their first date at 3 a.m. after they've both worked a long shift, or groups of people pounding tequila shots in honor of someone's birthday.

But it's not all wild nights filled with craziness here—though that's what they're known for.

There's also a really casual and cool jazz night that never fails to draw a crowd of locals every Tuesday, which coincidently is also a great time to sip your way through their natural wine list or to order some of the delicious tapas that you can't quite enjoy if you only visit during the chaotic late-night hours.

JAGUAR SUN

398 NE 5th Street
Miami, FL 33132

Jaguar Sun slid into the scene in 2018 and immediately stole the hearts of every cocktail lover in the Magic City. Helmed by Carey Hynes and Will Thompson, two dudes who decided to pack their bags and move to Miami to open a bar without ever living in the city, the mission here has always been to impress those coming to drink with the food and those coming to eat to leave equally impressed with the cocktails.

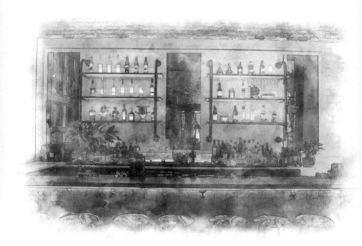

Mission accomplished. The menu features well-curated cocktails, ranging from a clarified passion fruit fino martini to a funky rhum agricole drink served in an astronaut rocks glass. To soak it all up there are Parker house rolls served with honey butter, oysters, and fresh made pastas.

While the cocktail program might be one of the most serious in Miami—Thompson is very particular about the brands he's willing to carry, the bar itself is one of the most chill vibes and their crowd of regulars can be seen sitting at the bar multiple times a week.

GREEN GHOUL

1 ½ oz. poblano-infused tequila

½ oz. mezcal

1 oz. fresh English cucumber juice

¾ oz. fresh lime juice

¾ oz. serrano pepper-infused simple syrup

1. Combine all of the ingredients in a cocktails shaker with ice, shake well, and strain into a margarita glass.
2. Garnish with a twisted cucumber ribbon.

MAMA TRIED

207 NE 1st Street
Miami, FL 33132

Mama Tried is almost designed to look like a dive bar, but it's definitely not one. Featuring red carpet and a wall emblazoned with the playfully misspelled "No Regerts," imbibers at this bar always find themselves having a great time. The U-shaped bar takes center stage as its ceiling features a starlit sky complete with shooting stars every few seconds.

The cocktail list runs eclectic and affordable with everything from fancy martinis to ice cold White Claw. It's the kind of place that works for both a quick happy hour after work or a late-night visit when you just want to take shots and dance your ass off.

There's a variety of DJs spinning hip-hop and classics, and on the last Sunday of the month, Mama Tried hosts a special treat for those who refuse to let go of their moody roots. Emo Night takes place from 10 p.m. until 5 a.m. and is easily the busiest night of the month at this beloved hotspot.

Tyler Kitzman is the bar manager/partner and has bartended at some of Miami's best bars under some of the world's best bartenders, including the legendary John Lermayer.

MAMA'S PORN STAR MARTINI

A Miami spin on this homage to Douglas Ankrah, creator of the Porn Star Martini.

2 oz. Absolut Vanilla

¾ oz. passion fruit puree

¾ oz. fresh pineapple juice

¾ oz. Licor 43

Pinch of Maldon sea salt

Sidecar of sparkling wine

1. Combine all of the ingredients in a cocktail shaker filled with ice, except for the sparkling wine, shake until chilled, and strain into a coupe.
2. Serve sparkling wine halfway up flute and garnish with a Filthy Cherry.

MARGOT NATURAL WINE BAR

21 SE 2nd Avenue
Miami, FL 33131

The folks from Bar Lab have made their mark on Downtown Miami with a natural wine bar that's unlike any other in town. Located in a loft-like space in the historic Ingraham Building, the vibe here is funky and mellow, much like the natural wines and low-ABV cocktails found on the menu. Named Margot after Ernest Hemingway's daughter, the spot is filled with girly pink hues and cozy corners ideal for drinking with friends or first dates.

Taking into consideration that natural wines are in the spotlight these days, the staff here is happy to rise to the occasion when it comes to explaining what's available as well as the tasting notes and mouth-feels of each wine.

The menu of small bites features sardines, cheeses, and oysters carefully curated to enhance your wine drinking experience. We love that Gabe Orta, Elad Zvi, and the entire Bar Lab team have ventured into wine world by creating a bar specializing in natural wines.

LOST BOY DRY GOODS

157 E Flagler Street
Miami, FL 33131

Founded in 2018, this neighborhood bar focuses on well-made cocktails and cold beers. This Downtown go-to resulted from a love "for a good English pub with the feel of an old Captain's tavern in a Colorado miner's saloon." Their cocktails lean heavily on classics, with ample beers on draught. It has also become somewhat of a haven for English football fanatics, opening as early as 7 a.m. to show all the big matches taking place across the pond. Being in the heart of the city, there is a great happy hour for the after-work crowd.

The space itself holds family memories for co-owner Randy Alonso, whose parents came from Cuba and opened a demin store of the same name in the same space. His partner, Chris Hundall, wanted to help preserve Alonso's family's space and put great attention and detail into the cocktails and operations, leading to the success of Lost Boy. Today it stands as one of the pioneer bars in this new era of Downtown Miami.

SEASONAL G+T

1½ oz. Portobello Road Gin

¼ oz. Mancino Secco Vermouth

East Imperial Grapefruit Tonic, to top

1. Combine the gin and vermouth in a goblet and top with the tonic.

2. Express a lemon peel over the cocktail and discard, and then add the Dehydrated Candied Lemon Wheel and a rosemary tip.

Dehydrated Candied Lemon Wheel: Preheat oven to 275°F. Cut 4 lemons into wheels and arrange on a parchment-lined baking sheet. Sprinkle ½ cup sugar over lemon wheels. Bake for 40 to 50 minutes, until lemons look like candy. Let cool and carefully peel off parchment paper.

BLACK MARKET

168 SE 1st Street
Miami, FL 33131

Created for locals by locals, this upscale sports bar with an unapologetic *Miami Vice* vibe is the place to root for local college and professional teams. With over thirty televisions gracing the walls, you won't miss any of the big sporting events, and you can rely on game-day specials, as well as a regular 2-for-1 happy hour special. Black Market became such a popular Downtown watering hole that they opened a second location in nearby Bayside Marketplace with the same ambiance in a waterfront setting.

If you're not rooting for a Miami team, then chances are you're going to be in the minority here as most of the patrons are diehard Dolphins or Canes fans.

THE TIPSY FLAMINGO

40 NE 1st Avenue, #101
Miami, FL 33132

"No flocks given." The motto is fitting since the flamingo theme runs heavy here. The neon tropical vibe instantly transports you out of the city center and into a soothing sea of inspired cocktails. The space itself draws from Miami's natural elements with a color palette of greens, purples, and hot pink with walls decorated in playful vintage palm leaf wallpaper and faux foliage.

The cocktail menu is an ode to Miami where each drink was designed to pay homage to and showcase the city's personality. From the Downtown Mentirita, the Tipsy Flamingo's version of the classical Cuba Libre, to the very popular "My English Is Not Very Good Looking," which tastes just like a pastelito de guayaba.

While there's no specific menu here, The Tipsy Flamingo has partnered with local spots to offer free delivery to the restaurant giving guests a range of options from Sam's Crispy Chicken to Krispy Rice and more.

OVER UNDER

151 E Flager Street
Miami, FL 33131

Really diving into all things Florida right down to an oversized mosquito—don't worry, he's drinking a martini and won't bite (oh yeah, and it's a neon sign). This spot can feel like it's got multiple personalities depending on the day and time you visit. Some days you might discover you're the only person at the bar and others you're fighting for a chance to order a beer and a shot while dozens of people sign up for late-night karaoke.

No matter when you go, Over Under is serving great drinks and equally wonderful food with favorites including the smoked fish dip and shell-tini, featuring oyster shell-infused gin. Pro tip: the veggie burger is so good, many meat-loving locals have gone as far as to say it's the best burger in the city.

NIU WINE

134 NE 2nd Avenue
Miami, Florida 33132

Owned and operated by Karina Iglesias, who Miami fell in love with thanks to Niu Kitchen (which is still just a few doors down), this low-key wine bar is the kind of place you go when you're looking to catch up with a friend or want to get to know someone on a first date.

You're not going to sit down in this super intimate space and stare at a basic wine menu. Niu Wine is all about figuring out your vibe, so you're more than likely going to chat with Iglesias or one of her other amazing sommeliers about what you're looking for. Then they're going to head into their fancy wine storage to pull a few options for you to try to ensure you're soon to be sipping on a wine that delights your taste buds and sets the mood—whether that's one of a romantic date night or a long Thursday at the office.

To complement the stellar wine selection there's also a small bites menu filled with charcuterie and more.

BAR LA REAL

100 NE 1st Avenue
Miami, FL 33132

There is a cocktail atmosphere, a speakeasy vibe, and a vintage tropical ambiance all wrapped into this beautifully designed bar housed in a 1917 historical building. Self-described as an "Ático Bar Tropiglam," Bar La Real brings inventive cocktails to a high-energy lounge in a way that Downtown Miami hasn't seen in years. When they're open, the party doesn't stop until 5 a.m.

While this leans more toward lounge, Bar La Real's attention to elixirs, including shrubs and infusions, makes the cocktails standout. As this is housed in a historic property, the attention to glassware is also important.

Owned and operated by White Feather Management, the team behind Wynwood's El Patio and Mayami Latin concepts, the goal is to emulate the opulence and elegance of the peacock frequently seen roaming around the streets of Coconut Grove.

THE AULD DUBLINER

91 NW 1st Street
Miami, FL 33128

Not quite what you'd expect at this gem of a bar in downtown Miami. Family-owned and operated, it opens early enough to serve the best Irish breakfast in town and stays open late enough to make it a solid spot to watch your favorite sports. The pints here are perfectly poured and their whiskey selection impressive. Spend a few hours inside and you'll forget you're in the middle of a tropical city.

CASA FLORIDA

437 SW 2nd Street
Miami, FL 33130

Nestled on the property of the oldest recorded hotel license in the city's history, Casa Florida brings you old Miami in a unique way. Vibrant cocktails are served out of a repurposed shipping container with a vintage canoe as a backbar, and a 1969 GM bus has been converted into a lounge. Add these singular touches to outdoor space ample enough to include a custom-made ping-pong table and two bocce courts, it's easy to see why this space is known as the Playground. Expect punches, fresh oysters, and playful riffs on classic cocktails. The original structures on the property date back to the early 1900s when this location was known as the Miami River Inn, and today they are on the National Register of Historic Places. Grab a cocktail and take a walk through Miami's past as you also celebrate the highly creative present.

CANOE CLUB

1½ oz. Ilegal Mezcal

½ oz. Crème de Mure

¾ oz. Ginger–Serrano Syrup

½ oz. fresh lime juice

3 dashes Peychaud's Bitters

1. Combine all of the ingredients in a cocktail shaker, stir to combine, add ice, and then shake.

2. Strain into a rocks glass over nugget ice.

Ginger–Serrano Syrup: Combine 2 parts sugar, 1 part water, 3 serrano peppers, and 2 large pieces of ginger in a saucepan over medium-high heat and cook until all of the sugar is dissolved. Keep cooking to taste—the longer it cooks, the spicier it will be—and then let cool, strain, and store.

Coconut Grove/ South Miami

A. **Fox's Lounge**
   6030 S Dixie Highway

B. **Bougainvillea's Old Florida Tavern**
   7221 SW 58th Avenue

C. **Barracuda**
   3035 Fuller Street

D. **Sandbar Sports Grill**
   3064 Grand Avenue

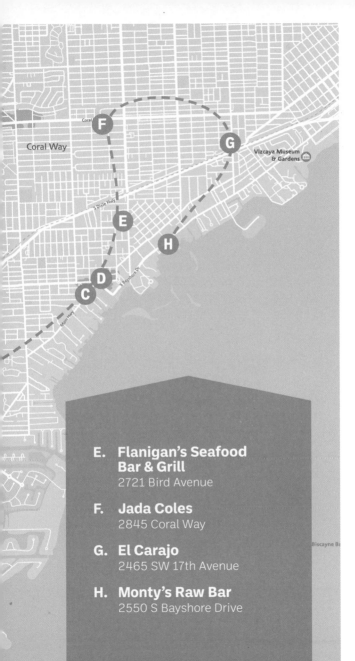

Coral Way

Vizcaya Museum
& Gardens

Biscayne Ba

E. **Flanigan's Seafood
   Bar & Grill**
   2721 Bird Avenue

F. **Jada Coles**
   2845 Coral Way

G. **El Carajo**
   2465 SW 17th Avenue

H. **Monty's Raw Bar**
   2550 S Bayshore Drive

FOX'S LOUNGE

6030 S Dixie Highway
South Miami, FL 33143

From 1946 until 2015, Fox's Lounge operated as a bar and restaurant with a cool takeaway window liquor store in South Miami. A favorite for students at the University of Miami, you'd often find them walking late at night down the sidewalk of US-1 in the days before Uber. It was a heartbreaking moment when its closure was announced and bar rats mourned the loss of this great bar.

But, fortunately for us, the folks from Lost Boy Dry Goods (see page 76) found a way to bring Fox's Lounge back to life and reopened the famed bar in 2022. Keeping true to the original bar with wood-paneled, red leather banquettes, nautical swivel bar chairs, red lighting, hand-painted signage, and even a 1960s juke-box, Miamians have been thrilled with the revival. The cocktail menu was given a minor facelift, but still serves the same caliber of great drinks we've all come to crave from this iconic space.

BOUGAINVILLEA'S OLD FLORIDA TAVERN

7221 SW 58th Avenue
South Miami, FL 33143

Located in the heart of South Miami, and lovingly known as "Bougie's" by locals, this bar has been through it all since first opening in 2000, including coming close to permanently closing a couple of times. Housed in an old Florida cottage that has been converted into a live music venue, the tavern is made of Dade County pine, which has been almost completely harvested and is often only found in older homes around town. Before it was a tavern, this cottage was a tearoom, a gift shop, and even a doctor's office.

Bougie's is all about solid drink options and a guaranteed good time. For those not looking for the average, sit at the bar and hang out experience, this bar's event calendar is a busy one with live music. It's the only bar of its kind in the suburbs of Miami that's open every night until 5 a.m. making it extra popular around holidays that tend to see lots of outings. For Halloween, St. Patrick's Day, and even the night before Thanksgiving, Bougie's will add extra bars and sometimes even takes over the full block with its epic parties.

BARRACUDA TAPHOUSE & GRILL

3035 Fuller Street
Coconut Grove, FL 33133

As you walk along Fuller Street, you'll notice the pink hues that make this friendly bar standout from the rest. Since 1995, beer has ruled at this Coconut Grove staple; at last check there were over fifty beers on tap—though the wine list and spirits are worthy, too.

Don't miss their mahi fish sandwich that's perfect to enjoy while watching the game or dropping cash in the jukebox. There's weekly karaoke and trivia that keeps familiar faces coming back to this casual watering hole.

The fairly recent permanent closure of Fuller Street to traffic has allowed its outdoor seating to spill out onto the street, which was a welcomed addition as this cozy bar gets crowded later into the night.

SANDBAR SPORTS GRILL

3064 Grand Avenue
Miami, FL 33133

This Coconut Grove institution has been around for over twenty years. It's weathered hurricanes, ownership changes, and even a fire. Once featured on Jon Taffer's *Bar Rescue*, Sandbar was transformed into something that didn't pass the Miami vibe check and certainly didn't belong in Coconut Grove. Fortunately, it was quickly reverted back to the Sandbar we know and love.

They serve self-proclaimed world-famous fish tacos (on Taco Tuesdays they're half off), host rowdy college nights, and play every sports game imaginable on their thirty televisions.

Those who remember Sandbar in Coconut Grove's heyday were fond of their Wednesday nights when you could get beers for a penny or 3 beers for a dollar, women would wrestle covered in chocolate pudding in inflatable children's pools, and there were pole dancing competitions where the winner would walk away with $500. What a time to be alive that was! Though it's calmed down quite a bit, it's still a favorite hangout spot for locals.

FLANIGAN'S SEAFOOD BAR & GRILL

2721 Bird Avenue
Miami, FL 33133

Flanigan's is without a doubt one of South Florida's most beloved institutions. Founded by Joe "Big Daddy" Flanigan, this family-friendly joint began humbly when it opened in 1959 and now boasts over twenty locations throughout the state.

Famous for their chicken wings, baby back ribs, rockin' rib rolls, and their big green plastic cups emblazoned with the bearded face of the founding father, Flanigan's serves food from lunch to late at night. With epic specials like lunches under $15, free nachos when you buy a pitcher, and half off everything at the bar after 9 p.m. every single day, it's not hard to figure out why Miami has embraced this place. Plus you can always count on them making sure to show all the important sports games.

Honestly, if you don't have at least one big green Flanigan's cup in your house, then you're not a real Miamian —bonus points if you have the limited edition pink cup that's featured every October in honor of Breast Cancer Awareness Month.

JADA COLES

2845 Coral Way
Miami, FL 33145

A neighborhood hangout with cocktails, live music, karaoke, pool, a poker night, and a solid daily happy hour.

Jada Coles is as easy to get to as it is to miss when driving down the tree-shaded section of Coral Way. It's a super laid-back bar with no line, no wait, and friendly service. Jam sessions are a big part of the vibe here with live music and open mic nights being what draws most people back.

There's not much to it and sometimes that's all you need.

EL CARAJO

2465 SW 17th Avenue
Miami, FL 33145

For years, El Carajo was one of Miami's best kept secrets as it hid inside an unassuming gas station right off of the eternally backed up US-1 highway.

In recent years the space has become popular enough that a sign has been added to the outside of the building. Serving Miami since 1981, this quaint space features amazing authentic Spanish tapas and 2,000 of the world's best wines. Don't know much about wine? The staff here is very knowledgeable and always willing to help you figure out the best choice for you.

You may know *carajo* to be considered a bad word, but it's come to have multiple meanings in Hispanic societies and can be used as part of many expressions. In fact, carajo might just be one of the most used words in the Spanish language and seems to be indispensable when it comes to Spanish vocabulary, according to the owners of El Carajo.

MONTY'S RAW BAR

2550 S Bayshore Drive
Miami, FL 33133

Miami does not lack waterfront spots. So, when you talk about Monty's, considered one of the best waterfront bars in town, you know you're in for something special. Under tiki huts in historic Coconut Grove, Monty's, opened by Monty Trainer (aka "The Grove Father"), has served guests since 1969. Their island cocktails and famous happy hour are legendary among Miamians, and their Pain Remover is a cult classic. If crazed mixology is what you're thirsty for, go elsewhere. But if you want to drink like a local, Monty's is the spot for you.

PAIN REMOVER

It doesn't matter what it's called on the menu, locals order this spiked punch by asking for a "PK3." The "3" means you want extra rum in your drink, which certainly helps wash away whatever pain ails you.

1½ oz. rum

½ oz. coconut cream

2 oz. orange juice

2 oz. pineapple juice

1. Combine all of the ingredients in cocktail shaker filled with ice, shake vigorously, and pour into a plastic cup.

Wynwood/Midtown

A. Dante's HiFi
519 NW 26th Street

B. Gramps
176 NW 24th Street

C. J. Wakefield Brewing
120 NW 24th Street

D. Kush Wynwood
2003 N Miami Avenue

E. Cerveceria La Tropical
42 NE 25th Street

F. Beaker & Gray
2637 N Miami Avenue

G. Grails
2800 N Miami Avenue

H. Lagniappe
3425 NE 2nd Avenue

I. Sylvester
3456 N Miami Avenue

DANTE'S HIFI

519 NW 26th Street
Miami, FL 33127

Inspired by intimate vinyl listening clubs that are popular in Japan, Dante's HiFi is lined with wall-to-wall records and 1970s wood-paneled basement vibes. The emphasis is unquestionably on the sound—the system is exceptional. The cocktails are tasty with a focus on highball drinks meant to be aligned with what you'd find in a Japanese listening club.

Open until 2 a.m. on the weekends. Dante's plays only vinyl, selecting from their curated collection of over 8,000 records. Rich Medina, the musical director, has traveled the world DJing the masses and has worked with artists like De La Soul, The Roots, and Femi Kuti, to name a few.

GRAMPS

176 NW 24th Street
Miami, FL 33127

With all the growth in Wynwood, Gramps is one of the original spots that makes the area feel less touristy and more like home.

It's got unique programming (think drag bingo, nerd night, holiday pop-up bars) and outstanding cocktails. The indoor bar serves up creative fresh cocktails while their lush, tropical outdoor patio serves as a backdrop for bands from all over the world. Tucked away on the patio is one of Miami's favorite pizza joints, Pizza Tropical.

Owner, Adam Gersten pays tribute to legendary Miami bars and restaurants like Flanigan's with small details throughout the space that amplify the seaside tavern aesthetic. Tables and fixtures are painted by local artists and friends that have made this bar as much about being picturesque as it is about the pizza and cocktails.

Gersten once said, "If we are a little bit Churchill's, a little bit Deuce, a little bit Bougainvillea's, a little bit The Corner, a little Jimbo's, and obviously a lot Gramps, then I think we are doing our job right."

GRAMPS OLD FASHIONED

If Miami had a signature Old Fashioned, it would be this one made with rum instead of whiskey.

2 oz. Brugal 1888

¼ oz. Black Pepper Syrup

2 dashes Angostura bitters

2 dashes orange bitters

1. Combine all of the ingredients in a mixing glass filled with ice and stir until chilled.
2. Strain over ice in a rocks glass and garnish with an orange peel.

Black Pepper Syrup: In a saucepan, combine 1 cup Demerara sugar, 1 cup water, and ½ oz. crushed black peppercorns and bring to a simmer. Remove from heat, let cool, strain, and store.

J. WAKEFIELD BREWING

120 NW 24th Street
Miami, FL 33127

Johnathan Wakefield discovered his passion for crafting beers as a home brewer before opening his own brewery right in the heart of the Wynwood Arts District. This brewery and tasting room serves some of the best beers in Miami.

Hop into the taproom for huge street art murals of your favorite sci-fi movies, mainly Star Wars, while classic movies play on the screen. In a neighborhood that has fast become a global art destination, J. Wakefield Brewing allows you to see and taste the respective art forms.

Always keeping the love of locals in mind, the brewery is host to several food pop-ups ranging from juicy smash burgers by Ted's Burgers to grilled cheese from Ms. Cheezious.

KUSH WYNWOOD

2003 N Miami Avenue
Miami, FL 33127

Matt Kuschner wanted to be a part of the local craft beer community while also celebrating the vibrant Wynwood arts scene. Boasting eighteen taps, a huge collection of rare bottled beers, and a from-scratch food menu that includes locally-sourced beef burgers, alligator bites, and Frito pie, Kush is a neighborhood favorite that gets international attention though it's only got a handful of seats.

Kuschner started his journey into entrepreneurship with Lokal in 2011. In 2014, Kush Wynwood came to life as a beer bar and he has continued to open bars and restaurants since then with attention to food and drink that is well known amongst locals. Also, off the beaten path, is La Cocina, a Cuban-inspired cocktail bar in Hialeah. Their focus is directed at the subculture of Miami and small details that only locals would know.

And that's what makes these spots so special. A local can tell you a story about what's on the wallpaper or about the picture framed on a wall.

CERVECERIA LA TROPICAL

42 NE 25th Street
Miami, FL 33137

In 1888, the Blanco-Herrera family established Cervecería La Tropical in Cuba. Considered Cuba's oldest brewery, it grew so popular that by 1958 La Tropical accounted for over 60 percent of all beer production in Cuba and had become a multinational brand. Cubans who were exiled longed to taste this beer once again.

After nearly a decade of research, Ramon Blanco-Herrera was able to gather enough information and the original recipe to open the ultimate tribute to his family—Cerveceria La Tropical, inviting customers back to pre-revolution Cuba with not only the La Original beer, but also an exciting Caribbean food menu and tasty Cuban-inspired cocktails.

"La Tropical founded the Cuban beer industry. La Tropical comprised acre upon acre of a brewery, tropical gardens, and a baseball stadium whose infield sand was made of crushed La Tropical bottles. There were many owners, but my family held majority ownership. As a kid, I loved going to the brewery with my father. I can still smell the sweet and thick malty scent coming from the brewery," shared Blanco-Herrera, fourth generation La Tropical family member and owner of Cerveceria La Tropical.

BEAKER & GRAY

2637 N Miami Avenue
Miami, FL 33127

Worldly cuisine and creative cocktails rule the night at Beaker & Gray. Two childhood friends, chef/co-owner Brian Nasajon and manager/co-owner Ben Potts, bring food and drink to Wynwood. Happy hour is Wednesday to Sunday, from 5 to 7 p.m. with a focus on bar snacks and craft cocktails.

The bar, designed by Potts, is set up in a way that it's not uncommon for curious imbibers to ask questions about the bottles displayed on the backbar. Luckily,

every bartender behind this stick is more than happy to answer your questions and help you to experiment with whatever you might be looking to try.

ROSE COLORED GLASSES

4 oz. rose

1 oz. Rosemary Syrup

¼ elderflower cordial

¼ oz. St-Germain

1 oz. fresh watermelon juice

¾ oz. fresh lemon juice

1 oz. soda water

1. Combine all of the ingredients, except the soda water, in a cocktail shaker with ice, shake well, and strain into a coupe over ice.

2. Add soda water and garnish with a rosemary sprig.

Rosemary Syrup: In a saucepan, bring 1 cup of water to a boil. Add 1 cup sugar and stir until clear. Remove from heat, add 1 tablespoon rosemary leaves, cover and let stand for 36 hours. Strain and store.

GRAILS

2800 N Miami Avenue
Miami, FL 33127

Do you love sports and sneakers? Then this is the spot for you. This bar is a culmination of all its owner's favorite things: sneakers, sports, and graffiti—which is a perfect fit in art-filled Wynwood. The walls are filled with glass display cases featuring some seriously coveted kicks (aka grails), including a limited edition pair of Back to the Future Nikes, while over seventy televisions hang in various places across the ceiling, both indoor and outdoor. If a game or fight is on, it's playing and you're going to want to arrive early because this place gets slammed with passionate fans who are ready to celebrate when whomever they are rooting for wins.

The bar food is elevated with dishes like cheeseburger dumplings, tuna tostadas, and loaded yuca fries. Several of their cocktails are actually served in porcelain sneaker-shaped vessels that are available for purchase. Opt for the tiny shot glass-sized drink or get crazy with the Holy Grail, which is coined as "one sneaker to rule them all" that holds twenty cocktails and is meant to be shared with a group of up to a dozen people, presented tableside.

SATISFY YOUR SOLE

The signature cocktail is a variation of a Moscow mule, using fresh cold-pressed watermelon juice, lemon verbena ginger-syrup, and a splash of soda. At the bar it is served in one of their sneaker-shaped vessels, so if you don't have one of those, use a rocks glass.

2 oz. Ketel One Vodka

¾ oz. lemon verbena-ginger syrup

¾ oz. fresh lime juice

¾ oz. watermelon juice

2 oz. soda water

1. Combine all of the ingredients, except the soda water, in a cocktail shaker with ice, shake well, and strain into a glass over ice.

2. Add the soda water and garnish with a dehydrated lime wheel, watermelon slice, and edible flower.

LAGNIAPPE

3425 NE 2nd Avenue
Miami, FL 33137

Lagniappe has been recognized as one of the country's top wine bars and we couldn't agree more. Owned by David Tunnell, who wanted to bring a New Orleans vibe (we get it, we've been to Bacchanal and love it, too!) to Miami.

Lagniappe is located in a former residential home that still hosts artists who need a place to crash in its upstairs rooms. They don't take reservations so you've got to be quick to snag a table.

Here's how it works: you arrive and send one person to commandeer a table, while another goes to the counter to check out the wine list and order snacks. Before you know it you'll be nice and cozy with your bottle (or two) of wine, a nice cheese plate, and lovely live music in the background.

Whether humid or chilly outside, Lagniappe brings music and wine lovers together in a gorgeous spot that is adored by both locals and tourists alike.

SYLVESTER

3456 N Miami Avenue
Miami, FL 33127

Helmed by the team behind nearby Beaker & Gray (see page 122), this dancey late-night lounge is a favorite for those who want to hang in Wynwood, but prefer to stick to its outskirts. There's a parking lot and plenty of seating (co-owner Ben Potts raided his parents storage and took a bunch of old school couches and comfy chairs) making it a great spot for those who want to pop in for a quick happy hour drink or a nightcap on the way home. The disco ball and DJ amp up the vibe while the bartenders mix up delicious libations using locally-sourced ingredients and Miami flair.

The younger crowd can be found on the couches and dancing throughout while industry folks tend to hang out a bit more at the bar, making it a favorite spot for local bartenders to visit after they've gotten off work.

VAXXXED & WAXXXED

½ oz. Don Julio

¼ oz. El Silencio Mezcal

¾ oz. Aperol

½ oz. Chinola Passion Fruit Liqueur

¼ oz. agave syrup

¾ oz. fresh lime juice

3 dashes spicy bitters

1. Combine all of the ingredients in a cocktail shaker with ice, shake well, and strain into a wine glass over ice.
2. Garnish with an orange slice and mint sprig.

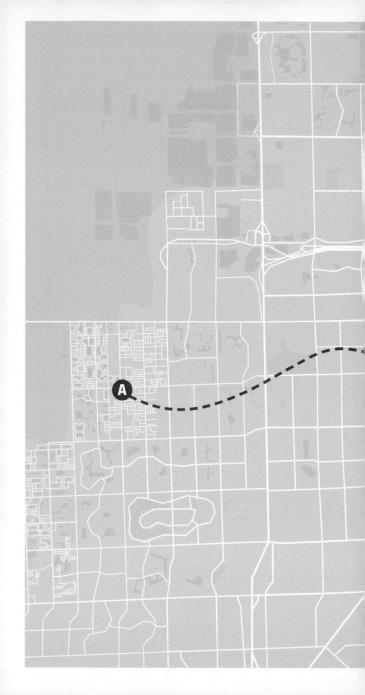

Kendall/Westchester/
Dadeland/Pinecrest

A. Finka Table & Tap
14690 SW 26th Street

B. La Mesa
8872 SW 24th Street

C. Abi Maria
8860 SW 72nd Place

D. Captain's Tavern
9625 South Dixie Highway

E. Keg South
10417 S Dixie Highway

FINKA TABLE & TAP

14690 SW 26th Street
Miami, FL 33175

This gastropub pioneered craft cocktails in Kendall. Chef Eileen Andrade's attention to food is seen in the cocktail menu as well, which features cult favorites that you'll never see leave the menu. If you're in the center of Miami, then this spot is likely out of your way, but worth the journey. The food is Cuban-Peruvian-Korean fusion. There is a strong focus on community with bartenders on staff that have been there since the beginning. Come hungry and thirsty.

Andrade's family has a long history in the restaurant world, including her mother, Nancy Andrade, who opened the legendary Isla Canarias in West Kendall.

Finka's bar is stocked with house-made syrups, fresh herbs, and esoteric brands that invite guests to ask questions.

BASIL-ANDO

The cucumber and grapefruit shine in this fresh and clean gin cocktail with the Cuban-inspired name. A Finka modern classic.

2 oz. Fifty Pounds Gin

¾ oz. fresh lemon juice

¾ oz. fresh cucumber juice

¾ oz. Grapefruit Syrup

Dash of Bittermens Boston Bittahs

1. Combine all of the ingredients in a cocktail shaker filled with ice and shake vigorously.
2. Double strain into a rocks glass over a large ice cube and garnish with 3 basil leaves.

Grapefruit Syrup: In a saucepan, combine a 2:1 ratio of simple syrup to fresh grapefruit juice; add a pinch of salt and a handful of rosemary. Bring to a boil and remove from heat. Strain, cool for 8 hours, label, and store.

LA MESA

8872 SW 24th Street
Miami, FL 33165

Located in the Westchester area of the city, the La Mesa mantra, "Cojelo suave," which loosely translates to "Take it easy," invites you to sit back, sip, and enjoy the vibe that is heavy with Latin and tropical influences. Along with the excellent food and drink menus, there is live music most nights. Unlike some of our neighborhoods where craft cocktail bars are everywhere, you don't find many of them in this area, and this one doesn't disappoint.

La Mesa has inspired a movement among bars and restaurants in the west side of Miami-Dade County to promote fresh ingredients, elevated food, and cocktails. As the neighborhood bar becomes the norm in South Florida, La Mesa is a welcome addition to this area of Miami.

ABI MARIA

8860 SW 72nd Place
Miami, FL 33156

Inspired by owner Jorgie Ramos's Cuban roots, the great tapas-style menu is accompanied by classic Cuban cocktails like the daiquiri and mojito. Downtown Dadeland needed a proper cocktail bar and this is it. The inviting space will remind you of what you've seen in vintage photographs from pre-revolution Cuba with a Miami twist, which makes total sense, since Ramos used a lot of his family's old furniture and decor.

Expect ingredients like mamey, guarapo, and passion fruit with an eclectic cocktail section. Ramos had been looking into opening a bar concept and succeed to do so with this spot. Since then, he's has expanded with his immensely popular Cebada Rooftop in the heart of Coral Gables.

And in 2019, he won Cochon 555, a cooking competition, focusing on heritage breed pigs, where he was crowned the 'Prince of Pork." That same year, his team entered the Art of Tiki Competition to win, yet again, Judge's Choice for the I Love Cuba Cocktail. This type of attention and hospitality is also at Bar Abi Maria.

CAPTAIN'S TAVERN

9625 South Dixie Highway
Miami, FL 33156

In 1971, Bill Bowers, aka "The Captain," opened the doors to this seafood shack in South Miami, and the look and the feel haven't changed since. The Captain himself described the interior design as "early depression." Wood-paneled walls are lined with nautical-themed artifacts and memories of The Captain. For fifty years, he kept prices low and created relationships with winemakers all over the world to create an experience unlike any other. You can come in for dinner, or just sit at the bar and talk to the locals who have called this their neighborhood bar for decades. The Captain left us in 2020, but his spirit still lives on.

Captain's Tavern works with seafood suppliers to search for the freshest product. They pride themselves on making everything in-house.

Captain's Tavern has been honored by *Food + Wine* magazine as one of "America's 50 Most Amazing Wine Experiences."

KEG SOUTH

10417 S Dixie Highway
Pinecrest, FL 33156

Keg South on US-1 has been a local favorite sports bar for cold beers and its famous grilled wings for over fifty years. It's home to Miami's Original Keg Burger, a classic backyard burger made with grade A beef, American cheese, and all the fixings.

It's a true neighborhood bar with a family feel. In fact, many of the people who work at the bar have been there for years or have followed in their family's footsteps first as a patron and then as an employee.

More than one patron has proclaimed it "a five-star dive bar"—it's hard to argue with enthusiastic regulars.

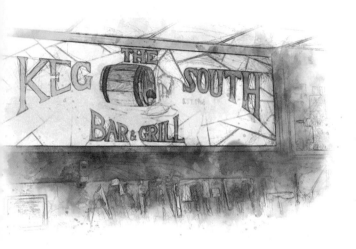

Little Havana

A. Bar Nancy
2007 SW 8th Street

B. Café La Trova
971 SW 8th Street

**C. Old's Havana
Cuban Bar & Cocina**
1442 SW 8th Street

**D. JC & Joanna's
Wine House**
5792 SW 8th Street

Dolphin Expy

Blue Lagoon

Joanne

Flagami

W Flagler St

SW 8th St

BAR NANCY

2007 SW 8th Street
Miami, FL 33135

When you think of Little Havana, your thoughts may immediately go to mojitos and Cuban music, but that's far from the case at Bar Nancy, a drinking establishment inspired by a ship that carried ammunition and spirits during the Revolutionary War.

Operating by the creed, "Carpe noctem," or "seize the night," through solid cocktails and great music, the bar is adorned with a ship-themed backbar as well as a colonial American flag.

The cocktails are nods to the high seas with delicious tropical drinks and spirit-forward beverages to keep you adrift on the good times.

With its hardcore all-American theme comes an eccentric crowd of motorcylce riders who enjoy rocking out to the classic rock cover bands that perform weekly.

CAFÉ LA TROVA

971 SW 8th Street
Miami, FL 33130

One of Miami's many well-loved Cuban restaurants, the bar at Café La Trova is led by Julio Cabrera, who is regarded as one of the most influential bartenders in the world. He brings his trademark Cantinero touch to Little Havana, where the bar team not only makes cocktails but plays along with the live band playing Trova, a genre of popular Cuban music.

This style of bartending brings back memories of pre-communist Cuba, where the show behind the bar reigned and bartenders were the stars. Co-owner and

James Beard Award-winner Michelle Bernstein designed the menu that includes Cuban hits like arroz con pollo and croquetas.

Quickly after opening, Café La Trova immediately started to be recognized by best bar lists from around the world. You can find Cabrera behind the bar making daiquiris or playing an instrument as he hosts guests with his signature style. His Cantinero ways have served him well on his bartending journey, even landing him on the cover of a special edition of *GQ* after he was crowned Bombay Sapphire's Most Imaginative Bartender in 2013.

BUENAVISTA

Julio Cabrera's legendary Buenavista is an award winner thanks to its refreshingly sublime blend of sweet and sour.

1½ oz. Bombay Sapphire

½ oz. St-Germain

½ oz. fresh lime juice

½ oz. simple syrup

¼ oz. cucumber juice

3-5 mint leaves

1. Combine all of the ingredients in a cocktail shaker with ice, shake well, and double strain into a chilled cocktail glass.
2. Garnish with a cucumber wheel and a mint leaf.

OLD'S HAVANA CUBAN BAR & COCINA

1442 SW 8th Street
Miami, FL 33135

This notable Little Havana bar has captured the hearts and minds of locals and tourists alike with vibrant art, great Cuban food, music and dance, and delicious cocktails.

The walls are decorated with historical memorabilia that speak to the glory days of Havana while the mahogany bar is decorated with vintage Coca Cola pendant lighting.

What's more impressive is the number of mojitos they serve per day—over 200—and they pride themselves on being "la casa de los mojitos."

Listen to live Cuban music in the afternoon, cozy up in the hidden backyard patio, and order a hearty Cuban dinner. You'll thank us later.

JC & JOANNA'S WINE HOUSE

5792 SW 8th Street
Miami, FL 33144

Formerly known as Happy Wine, this wine bar has over 1,000 wines and a tasty tapas menu all found in the laid-back ambiance of a wine warehouse. Grab a stool, set your wine on top of a wine barrel, and enjoy the music.

If you buy a bottle to enjoy before going home, they'll open it for you at the counter. As it gets later in the day, you'll notice locals start to roll in and order several tapas, like jamon serrano and Manchego cheese, croquetas, and tortilla Española to nosh on as they sip their favorite vintages.

Owned by Juan Carlos Restrepo and his wife Joanna Fajardo, this wine shop is their way of living out the American dream. This dream hasn't been without its struggles, as the couple once had a second location in Coconut Grove, but had to sell it in order to fund a kidney transplant for JC. Still, the couple continues to welcome everyone into the shop as though they are welcoming them into their home with a smile, a hug, and a wine opener in hand.

Little River/Little Haiti/ North Miami

A. **Paradis Books & Bread**
12831 W Dixie Highway

B. **Off Site**
8250 NE 2nd Avenue

C. **Phuc Yea**
7100 Biscayne Boulevard

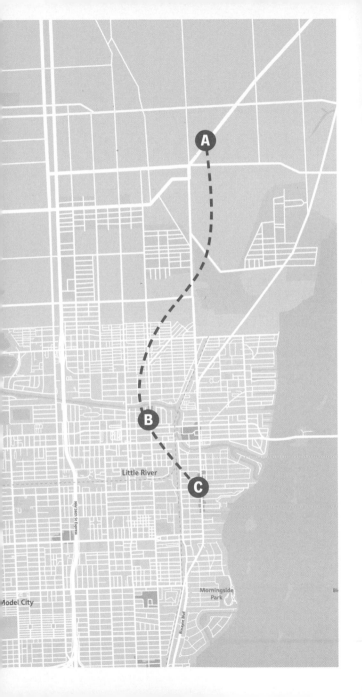

PARADIS BOOKS & BREAD

12831 W Dixie Highway
North Miami, FL 33161

Paradis Books & Bread's own description says it all: "Rad books, wine bar, sour dough, North Miami." Owned and operated by a group of New York friends who all have different hospitality backgrounds, this part wine shop/part bookstore has become somewhat of a community library.

With a focus on independent publishers and subjects like Black studies, critical theory, and international struggle and solidarity movements, this place is set up to spark conversations over good food and drink.

The wine program is defined by farmer-focused, expressive, vibrant, living wine. That means hand-harvested grapes, and no chemicals, pesticides, or herbicides in the vineyard, not to mention small production and small vineyards, indigenous yeasts that naturally start fermentation, and minimal to no additional sulfites.

Similarly the bakery program focuses on wholesome, naturally leavened breads and baked goods.

OFF SITE

8250 NE 2nd Avenue
Miami, FL 33138

This nanobrewery in the Little River area of Miami is owned by a couple of hospitality veterans who have put their blood, sweat, and tears into Miami's dining scene. Steve Santana and Adam Darnell have knocked it out of the park with this fun spot. They've figured out the perfect marriage of good food and good beer.

Serving American-style dishes and a large menu of both local and uniquely funky beers (in addition to those made on-site), it's a casual spot where it almost feels like everyone hanging out is really just one big group of friends.

There's a couple can't miss menu items you've got to try, including the Super Good Chicken sandwich that first debuted when Santana hosted a pop up at Darnell's former establishment, and the Super Good Lager, which is brewed specifically to pair with the infamous chicken sandwich.

PHUC YEA

7100 Biscayne Boulevard
Miami, FL 33138

This Vietnamese-Cajun mash-up owned by Cesar Zapata and Ani Meinhold was the first official pop-up Miami ever had the chance to experience and over a decade later remains one of the most homegrown concepts in the city.

"Phuc" is defined as "blessings and prosperity" in the Urban Dictionary, making this a fun play on words to describe the delicious cuisine that pairs perfectly with their chef-driven cocktails.

The happy hour is solid, and you'll be happy sipping from the drink menu inside or outside at this MiMo district spot. Cocktails are curated by Ani Meinhold, who doubles as both general manager and owner.

The cozy vibe and lo-fi soundtrack make this one of those places where you innocently end up for brunch, but find yourself several cocktails deep and still hanging out long enough to stay for dinner.

Must-order dishes include the crispy pork masitas made using five-spice roasted pork shoulder, nuoc cham, lemongrass chili, lime, onion, tomato, and herbage; and the PY noodles made with fresh noodles, fish sauce, and parm. As for cocktails, just stay until you've tried them all... seriously, they're that good.

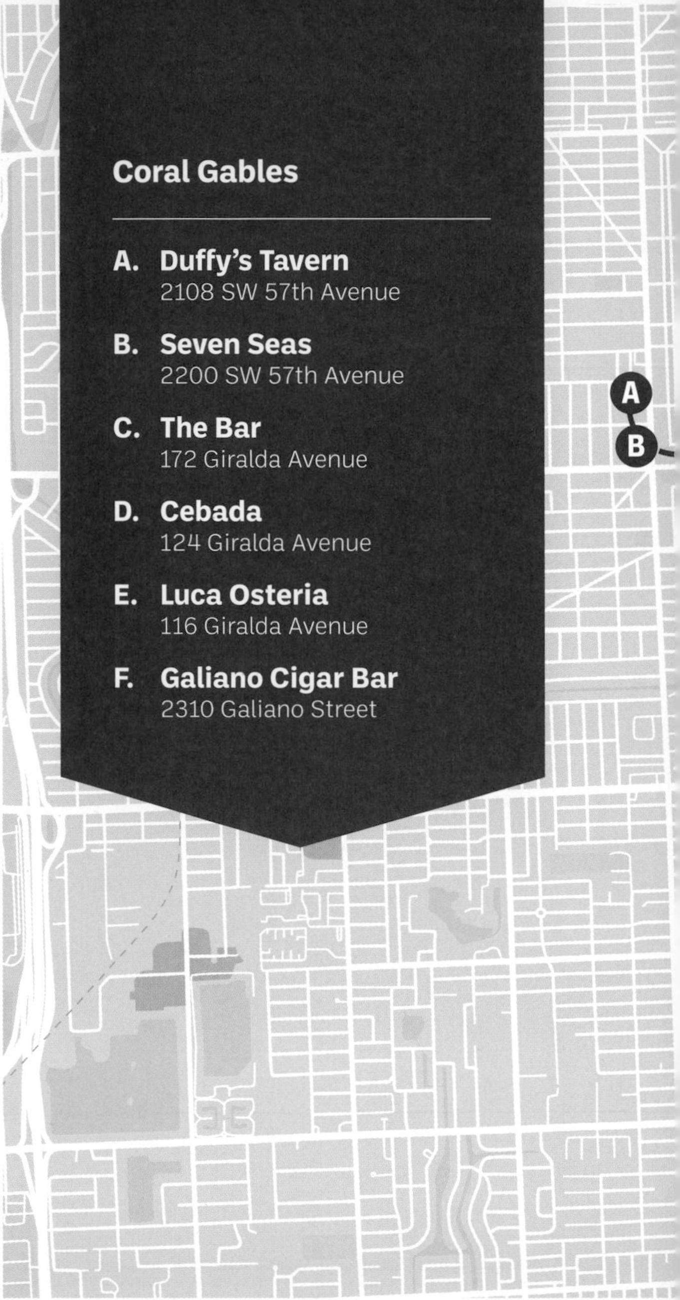

Coral Gables

A. Duffy's Tavern
2108 SW 57th Avenue

B. Seven Seas
2200 SW 57th Avenue

C. The Bar
172 Giralda Avenue

D. Cebada
124 Giralda Avenue

E. Luca Osteria
116 Giralda Avenue

F. Galiano Cigar Bar
2310 Galiano Street

A

B

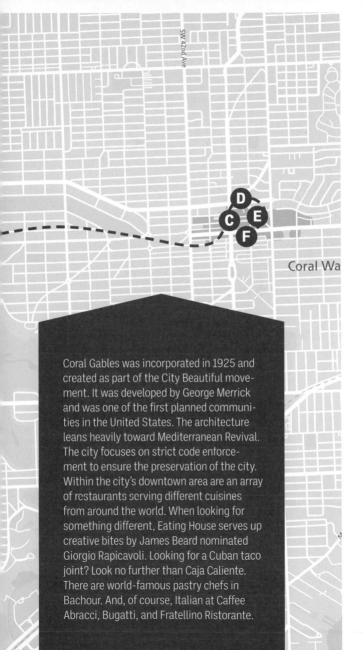

SW 42nd Ave

Coral Wa

Coral Gables was incorporated in 1925 and created as part of the City Beautiful movement. It was developed by George Merrick and was one of the first planned communities in the United States. The architecture leans heavily toward Mediterranean Revival. The city focuses on strict code enforcement to ensure the preservation of the city. Within the city's downtown area are an array of restaurants serving different cuisines from around the world. When looking for something different, Eating House serves up creative bites by James Beard nominated Giorgio Rapicavoli. Looking for a Cuban taco joint? Look no further than Caja Caliente. There are world-famous pastry chefs in Bachour. And, of course, Italian at Caffee Abracci, Bugatti, and Fratellino Ristorante.

DUFFY'S TAVERN

2108 SW 57th Avenue
Miami, FL 33155

Open since 1955, this is one of those neighborhood bars that everybody knows. Its tagline, "Come for the burgers and stay for the pints," is something that has been enjoyed by generations of locals.

It sits on the border of Coral Gables, but attracts patrons from all over, because they serve a mean burger and an even better pint. But the real secret to this joint's success? Celebrating community and bringing people together around good times and great conversations.

Explore the walls that feature an array of antiques and relics from Miami's yesteryear. But make sure to bring cash, because they won't accept credit cards, though there is an ATM onsite.

SEVEN SEAS

2200 SW 57th Avenue
Miami, FL 33155

This nautical-themed karaoke dive bar is not for the shy. There's no question that Seven Seas is one of the most popular karaoke joints in the Magic City.

Simple cocktails, beers on tap, and a pool table highlight this watering hole, but don't expect to hang out and not sing. Regulars here have a keen eye on who hasn't gone up yet and are always happy to help you with a little extra liquid courage if it means you'll get on stage to belt one out.

THE BAR

172 Giralda Avenue
Coral Gables, FL 33134

The Bar opened in 1946, and while plenty has changed over the years, one constant has been its status as a local favorite.

While the bar itself is pretty old, the crowd you'll find inside definitely isn't. Full of Millennials and Gen-Zers, this spot gets super busy during happy hour (drinks are 2-for-1) and on Fridays when ladies drink free.

It's a reliable place to go for classic bar food and karaoke, but don't be shocked if you run into those people you've been trying to avoid since high school.

CEBADA

124 Giralda Avenue
Coral Gables, FL 33134

Coral Gables' first-ever rooftop bar opened in 2021 after being teased (and constantly worked on) for three years. The moment doors opened, locals flocked to this lively spot where they can enjoy picturesque views of the Coral Gables skyline.

The tropical cocktails are named after Miami-inspired memories from owner Jorgie Ramos's childhood that read a bit like inside jokes—like "Every Belen Guy's Christmas Vacation," made with cucumber, ginger, honey, lemon, and Breckenridge Gin, because everyone knows a dude from Belen who won't stop talking about their ski trip.

Located on pedestrian-only Giralda Avenue, it's the perfect spot to start a night of hopping around the neighborhood's other great bars and restaurants.

Shared plates are the norm at Cebada, which encourages the act of having a drink and breaking bread with friends. From chicharrones de pato to dressed oysters, everything on the menu features a bit of the elevated Cuban-American twist that Ramos is known for.

LUCA OSTERIA

116 Giralda Avenue
Coral Gables, FL 33134

Luca Osteria is a quaint Italian restaurant located on the pedestrian-friendly Giralda Avenue in the heart of Coral Gables. Owned by Giorgio Rapicavoli, Miami's first Chopped winner, the menu features riffs on the recipes he grew up with as a child.

With a full bar and an extensive cocktail menu, it's the ideal setting for Italy's libations—spritzes, martinis, and aperitifs. Known for making one of the best espresso martinis around, this is the kind of spot where locals come when they're looking for a quick drink before dinner nearby or happily dine often for special occasions or just because they're craving fresh made pasta.

NEGRONI LUCA

1 oz. Bombay Dry Gin

1 oz. Contratto Aperitif

½ oz. Pierre Ferrand Dry Curacao

½ oz. Carpano Bianco Vermouth

4 dashes orange bitters

1. Combine all of the ingredients in a mixing glass with ice, stir, and train into a rocks glass over a large ice cube.

2. Express an orange twist over the cocktail and serve.

GOOD PASTA, GOOD PEOPLE

LUCA

OSTERIA

GALIANO CIGAR BAR

2310 Galiano Street
Coral Gables, FL 33134

This Coral Gables gem allows you to pick a cigar, order an old fashioned, and enjoy the lounge ambiance with the locals who have been coming in day after day for years. Expect classic cocktails and experts offering pairings on the extensive cigar and whiskey selections. Often times you might catch educators from cigar or spirit brands who are happy to lead you through tastings and pairings. If you enjoy a good cigar and a glass of whiskey, this is the spot for you.

Their inviting bar allows you to catch locals talking business and drinking rare spirits. At the center of Galiano Cigar Bar is a walk-in, temperature-controlled humidor where you can find your favorite cigars as well as local brands. If you make it up north, Ozzie Gomez is also owner of Downtown Cigar Bar in Fort Lauderdale. If Ozzie is not in, ask for Ciro, who is highly knowledgeable about the cigar and spirit selection.

Village of Key Biscayne

A. The Wetlab
4600 Rickenbacker Causeway

B. The Cleat
Unnamed Road

Biscayne Bay

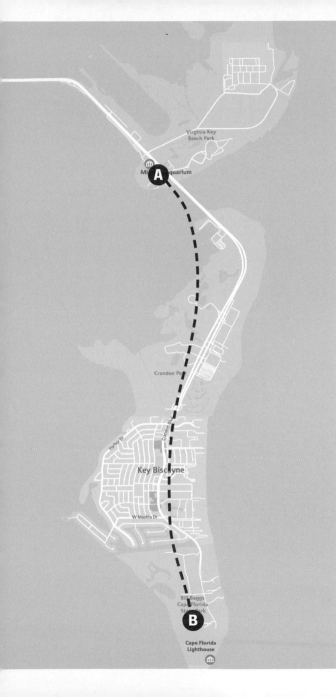

THE WETLAB

4600 Rickenbacker Causeway
Key Biscayne, FL 33149

Located within the University of Miami's Rosientiel School of Marine and Atmospheric Science, next to the Miami Sequarium on Biscayne Bay, is one of Miami's best kept secrets: The Wetlab. It's only open to the public Wednesday through Friday, and it might take you a bit to actually locate the bar, since you'll have to walk through the campus and past several classrooms. Once you've found it you'll be rewarded with enviable views of Biscayne Bay.

Aside from the gorgeous atmosphere (especially if you visit during sunset) this is a no-frills spot, in the best way possible. Just sit back and relax while student bartenders pour you one of fifteen craft beers on tap as you enjoy the live music.

THE CLEAT

Unnamed Road
Key Biscayne, FL 33149

A bit off the beaten path, in Key Biscayne, you'll have to make your way through Bill Baggs State Park to find this bar. You're coming here mainly because you want the feeling of sitting at the end of an island with breathtaking views on three sides of you. Show up by car, on foot, by bike, or even by sailboat.

Opened by a local, The Cleat is a family-owned labor of love where everyone knows the importance of a cold drink on a hot day. This is a one-of-a-kind, beautifully designed spot that will make you feel like you're in the know even if you're making your first-ever visit to the Magic City. Grab a cocktail, enjoy the sunset, and be thankful you're not paying crazy bottle service prices to enjoy this top-notch view.

Miami is known as the Magic City for a reason—the wonderful melting pot of cultures that can be found throughout the 305. Make your way into any neighborhood and you're bound to find an array of options stemming from different backgrounds and tastes.

While it's nearly impossible to fit everything Miami's hospitality scene has to offer in just a few pages, here's a solid start.

Frita Cubana

Fritas are a staple dish in Miami's culinary culture. These fast Cuban-style burgers are perfect before or after a long night on the town. With origins that date back to the 1930s in Cuba, this flavorful snack consists of a burger patty that's part ground beef, part chorizo seasoned with paprika and cumin. It's topped with crunchy shoestring fried potatoes and served on a fluffy Cuban bread roll. Sometimes there's cheese or condiments, but keeping it classic means you skip any additions.

Places to Go:
El Rey de las Fritas
Ariete
La Palma
Palomilla Grill
Amelia's 1931
Cuban Guys
Fritas Domino La Original
El Mago de las Fritas

Mojitos

Okay, so we didn't invent the mojito, but we do love calling it our official drink. Made with rum, sugar, and lime, the key is to keep it in balance.

Places to Go:
Mango's Tropical Cafe
Ball & Chain
Havana 1957
Esquina De La Fama
Cubaocho Museum and Performing Arts Center
Cafe La Trova
The Regent Cocktail Club
SUGARCANE Raw Bar Grill

Margaritas

In the city of eternal summer, margaritas are the ultimate refresher.

Places to Go:
Sweet Liberty
Bodega Taqueria y Tequila
Taquiza
Pilo's Tequila Garden
Rocco's Tacos & Tequila Bar
Tacology
Coyo Taco
Cantina La Veinte
Bakan

Burgers

Fun fact: Miami knows its way around burgers. From simple and juicy to massive and over-the-top, here are some of the best.

Places to Go:
Ariete
Pincho Factory
Blue Collar
United States Burger Service (USBS)
LoKal
Hole in the Wall
Proper Sausages
Bryson's Irish Pub
Cheeseburger Baby
Ted's Burgers
Silverlake Bistro

Cafecitos

Have you tried Miami's version of an energy drink? Roll up to one of Miami's "ventanitas" (small takeout windows) for a midday pick-me-up. It's a ritual that is shared by many Miamians, and is celebrated every day at 3:05 p.m.

Places to Go:
El Exquisito
La Carreta
Sergio's Restaurant
Vicky Bakery
Versailles Cuban Bakery
Polo Norte
Islas Canarias Bakery

Cuban Food

When someone visits a local in Miami, their first question more times than not is, "Where do I get good Cuban food?" Honestly, your best bet is to find someone's abuela to cook for you, but if that's not an option, here's where you want to go.

Places to Go:
Islas Canarias Bakery
Sergio's Cuban Café
Vicky Bakery
Palomilla Grill
Polo Norte
Morro Castle
Las Palmas
Versailles Cuban Bakery
La Carreta
El Exquisito
El Palacio de los Jugos

Colombian Food

In a city filled with late night drinking, you're going to need some late night snacking and Colombian food always fits the bill.

Places to Go:
La Estacion Cafe
El Patio 305
Patacon Pisao
Rincón Antioqueño Restaurant
El Palacio de los Frijoles
Pueblito Viejo
Los Arrieros
La Ventana Restaurant
Manantial Market Place
Sanpocho Restaurant

Hot Dogs

Hot dogs are one of America's favorite foods, and in Miami we like to put our own twist on them.

Places to Go:
Sweet Dogs 305
Los Verdes
Pincho Factory
Arbetter's Hot Dogs
Los Perros

Breweries

Much like the rest of the country, Miami has seen major growth when it comes to local breweries. From stouts to IPAs made with local fruits, there's no shortage of cool brews in this city.

Places to Go:
Veza Sur Brewing Co.
Lincoln's Beard Brewing Co.
Beat Culture Brewing
M.I.A. Beer Company
The Tank Brewing Co.
J. Wakefield Brewing
Wynwood Brewing Company
Cerveceria La Tropical
Spanish Marie Brewing
Tripping Animals Brewing Co.
Unbranded Brewing Co.

Ice Cream and Gelato

It's always summer in Miami and with temperatures well into 90°F and humidity at an all-time high, ice cream is always a good idea.

Places to Go:
Azucar Ice Cream Company
Cream Parlor
Whip'n Dip Ice Cream Shop
AUBI & RAMSA
Bianco Gelato
Wynwood Parlor
Crybaby Creamery
Sweet Melody Ice Cream
Dasher & Crank
Miami Coppelia Ice Cream

Bakeries

Sure everyone is focused on their bikini bodies here in Miami, but that doesn't stop us from having a serious sweet tooth. When it comes to desserts and baked goods, here's where to find the best.

Places to Go:
OH MY GOSH! Brigadeiros
Fireman Derek's Bakeshop
Cindy Lou's Cookies
Night Owl Cookies
Rolled
The Salty Donut
Mojo Donuts & Fried Chicken

Tacos

Who doesn't love tacos? It's the perfect hand-held food. Fortunately, there's no shortage of solid tacos in this town.

Places to Go:
Taquiza
Tacology
Coyo Taco
Jacalito Taqueria Mexicana
Huahua's Taqueria
El Taquito
The Taco Stand
Talkin' Tacos
Tacos El Carnal

Liquor Stores

When it comes to making cocktails at home, you're going to want to know what liquor stores you can truly count on to have what you need.

Places to Go:
Sunset Corners
Vintage Liquor
Crown Wine & Spirits
Big Game Liquors
Jensen's Liquor

Cigar Shops

Old Fashioneds and dominos pair well together, but if you want the true Miami trifecta, you're gonna need a damn good cigar.

Places to Go:
Stogie's Fine Cigars
Neptune Cigars
Little Havana Cigar Factory
Cuban Crafters
Padrón Cigars
Casa De Montecristo by Prime Cigar & Whiskey Bar
Art District Cigars
Gables Cigars
Coco Cigars
Aficionados Brickell

About Cider Mill Press
Book Publishers

Good ideas ripen with time. From seed to harvest,
Cider Mill Press strives to bring fine reading,
information, and entertainment together between
the covers of its creatively crafted books. Our Cider
Mill bears fruit twice a year, publishing a new crop of
titles each spring and fall.

"Where good books are ready for press"
501 Nelson Place
Nashville, Tennessee 37214

cidermillpress.com

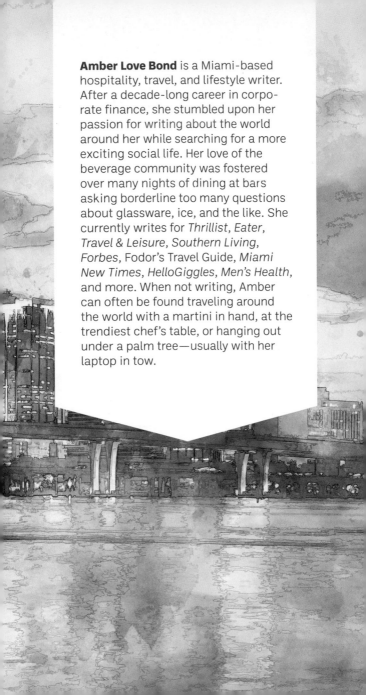

Amber Love Bond is a Miami-based hospitality, travel, and lifestyle writer. After a decade-long career in corporate finance, she stumbled upon her passion for writing about the world around her while searching for a more exciting social life. Her love of the beverage community was fostered over many nights of dining at bars asking borderline too many questions about glassware, ice, and the like. She currently writes for *Thrillist*, *Eater*, *Travel & Leisure*, *Southern Living*, *Forbes*, Fodor's Travel Guide, *Miami New Times*, *HelloGiggles*, *Men's Health*, and more. When not writing, Amber can often be found traveling around the world with a martini in hand, at the trendiest chef's table, or hanging out under a palm tree—usually with her laptop in tow.